Did You Know?
NEWCASTLE
& TYNESIDE

A MISCELLANY

Compiled by Julia Skinner
With particular reference to the work of Clive Hardy

THE FRANCIS FRITH COLLECTION

www.francisfrith.com

Based on a book first published in the United Kingdom in 2006 by The Francis Frith Collection®

This edition published exclusively for Identity Books in 2012 ISBN 978-1-84589-386-6

Text and Design copyright The Francis Frith Collection®
Photographs copyright The Francis Frith Collection® except where indicated.

The Frith® photographs and the Frith® logo are reproduced under licence from
Heritage Photographic Resources Ltd, the owners of the Frith® archive and trademarks.
'The Francis Frith Collection', 'Francis Frith' and 'Frith' are registered trademarks of
Heritage Photographic Resources Ltd.

British Library Cataloguing in Publication Data

Did You Know? Newcastle and Tyneside - A Miscellany
Compiled by Julia Skinner
With particular reference to the work of Clive Hardy

The Francis Frith Collection
Oakley Business Park,
Wylye Road, Dinton,
Wiltshire SP3 5EU
Tel: +44 (0) 1722 716 376
Email: info@francisfrith.co.uk
www.francisfrith.com

Printed and bound in Malaysia

Front Cover: **NEWCASTLE UPON TYNE, GRAINGER STREET 1900** N16314p

The colour-tinting is for illustrative purposes only, and is not intended to be historically accurate

CONTENTS

INTRODUCTION

The settlements that have developed around the mouth of the River Tyne lie in an area steeped in history, which was once part of the powerful Anglo-Saxon kingdom of Northumbria; but in around AD120, centuries before the Anglo-Saxons came here, Roman soldiers were building a great defensive wall out of stone and turf that spanned the entire width of Britain from Bowness on the west coast to Wallsend on the east, a distance of 73 miles. What is now known as Hadrian's Wall was created to prevent military invasions from the north by the Pictish tribes of Caledonia. It was the northern border of the Roman Empire in Britain for hundreds of years, and was certainly the most heavily defended fortification in the Empire. Surviving sections of Hadrian's Wall can be seen on the outskirts of Newcastle at Denton, on the A69.

The original New Castle on the Tyne was built by Robert Curthose, the brave but short tempered and headstrong eldest son of William the Conqueror, on his return from campaigning against Malcolm III of Scotland. It was a motte and bailey: a wooden tower on a mound was protected by a ditch on its west side and by precipitous banks on the other three, and it was from this fortification that Newcastle would derive its name. This castle was replaced by a stone castle in the late 12th century.

Agriculture, fishing and coalmining provided a livelihood in the area for many centuries. Charles I ensured Newcastle's prosperity when he granted the town the east of England coal trading rights, but this monopoly was to the detriment of nearby Sunderland, and the Tyne-Wear rivalry that ensued still exists. In the 18th century Newcastle became an important print centre, ranking with London, Oxford and Cambridge; the Literary and Philosophical Society of 1793, with its debates and large stock of books in several languages, predated the London Library by 50 years. Newcastle also became an important glass producer, and there was a rope-making industry here. However, Tyneside really boomed in the 19th century, becoming the industrial and commercial capital of the north-east, its wealth stemming from coal, iron and steel.

The shipbuilding industry around the River Tyne employed thousands of people. At the beginning of the 20th century British shipyards were at the forefront of both world shipbuilding and ship repairing, and could build a battleship twice as fast as any American yard, and five times faster than the embryonic Japanese shipbuilding industry. The economic depression of the 1930s caused a rapid decline in shipbuilding business and hit the area particularly hard, resulting in high levels of unemployment and great hardship.

In its heyday, Tyneside was a hive of heavy industry. There were dozens of coalmines working, shipyards lined the banks of the Tyne, railway locomotives were being built at Gateshead, and armoured vehicles were being made at Elswick. Nowadays much of this has gone, but has been replaced by modern factories, and there are new housing estates instead of pit heaps, winding gear and rows of miners' cottages.

'Canny Newcassel' looks forward into the 21st century as a vibrant, exciting and modern commercial city, but its history, and indeed that of all the settlements along the Tyne, is full of fascinating characters and events, of which this book can only provide a brief glimpse.

LOCAL DIALECT WORDS AND PHRASES

'Canny' - pleasant, kind, good.

'Deeky' - look at.

'Ken' - know.

'Bairn' - child.

'Hinny' - woman.

'Hacky' - dirty.

'Marra' - mate, friend.

'Clarts' - mud,   **'Clartin'** - messing about.

'Fernietickles' - freckles.

'Galluses' - men's braces.

'Plodge' - wade in water.

'Sanddancers' - The slang term for people from South Shields, a term that derives partly from the fact that the town boasts an attractive beach, and partly from its Yemeni population, the largest outside Yemen itself.

There is a long tradition of markets in Newcastle, which is continued by the weekend quayside market of present times. Some of the historical markets gave their names to parts of the city centre, such as Hay Market and Bigg Market (bigg was a form of barley); other markets were the Herb Market, the Cloth Market and the Butter Market. Paddy's Market was for second-hand clothes, and was so popular that it has given its name to a local phrase to describe somewhere busy and crowded: **'It's like Paddy's Market!'**

HAUNTED NEWCASTLE AND TYNESIDE

The ghost of Henry Hardwick is said to haunt the alleyways near the Cooperage public house. He was murdered trying to escape the press gang, and returns to haunt the spot where he died. Another ghost, of a man dressed in early 20th-century clothes, is also said to haunt this area.

Newcastle's Theatre Royal is said to be haunted by the ghost of a young lady who fell in love with an actor who had been performing in a play at the theatre. They met every evening after the play, and she was led to believe that he would marry her. However, when she arrived with her belongings before the final performance of the play, ready to run away with the actor, he told her that their affair was over. The distraught young lady sat in her usual place in the theatre gallery, and when the actor appeared on the stage she cried out to him and leant over the balcony; she either lost her balance and fell, or threw herself over, to her death. Her spirit, known as the Grey Lady of the Gallery, has haunted the theatre ever since.

Denton Hall on West Road, Newcastle, which is now the Bishop's House, home of the Roman Catholic Bishop of Hexham and Newcastle, has a ghost story associated with it. The ghost is believed to be that of a lady who was strangled by her jealous sister in the 17th century. A young lady staying in the hall reported seeing an old lady who came into her room and spoke to her, before disappearing with a sound like rustling silk, leaving her bedroom door locked; when she mentioned this to her hosts, she was told she had been visited by 'Old Burberry', who also wandered the grounds.

In the graveyard at Tynemouth Priory is a 'monk stone', where the ghosts of monks are said to come to pray. They are said to wear long brown gowns, with yellow belts, and with hoods with yellow markings.

NEWCASTLE AND TYNESIDE MISCELLANY

St Nicholas's Church in Newcastle was the fourth largest parish church in England until it became a cathedral in 1882, when Newcastle was awarded city status. A small part of the cathedral is late 12th-century, but most of the architecture is from the 14th and 15th centuries.

Medieval Newcastle was protected by a town wall with six main gateways: Sand Gate, West Gate, New Gate, Pandon Gate, Pilgrim Gate, and Close Gate. Along the wall were seventeen towers, and there were also a number of small turrets between the towers and gates which acted as lookout posts. The 16th-century antiquarian John Leland was most impressed with Newcastle's defences, describing them as 'far passing all the waulls of the cities of England and most of the cities of Europe'. Today the best surviving section of the old town wall to be seen is to the west of the city centre in the vicinity of Stowell Street; the remains of four towers may also be seen along this section of the defences. There is a smaller section of wall near Forth Street behind the Central Station, but nothing has survived of the walls to the north of Newcastle, and only three isolated towers remain to the east.

An important Anglo-Saxon monastery was founded at Jarrow in AD681 by Benedict Biscop. This is where the monk who became known as the Venerable Bede lived and worked (AD673-735). Bede is famous for being the first serious English historian, and his work 'The Ecclesiastical History of the English People' is valuable source material for historians of this period.

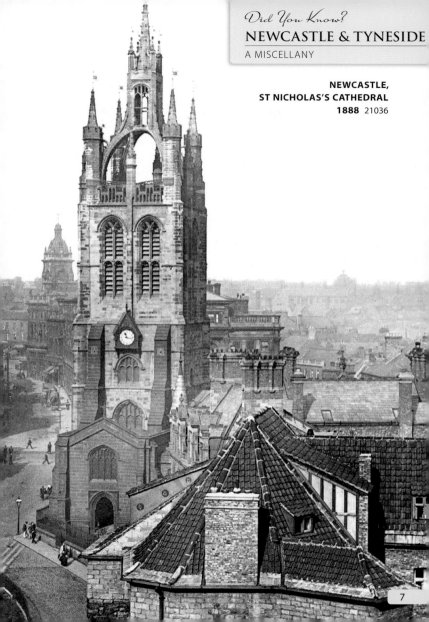

**NEWCASTLE,
ST NICHOLAS'S CATHEDRAL
1888** 21036

NEWCASTLE, FROM RABBIT BANKS c1898 N16304

The view of Newcastle shown in photograph N16304 (above) was taken from the Gateshead side of the river. Until 1800 Gateshead comprised little more that three main streets and was the northern end of the County Palatine of Durham. A third of the way along the old bridge over the Tyne were two blue stones; these marked the northern boundary of the Bishop of Durham's jurisdiction.

On the coast, Seaton Sluice is a small natural harbour once known as Hartley Harbour. A problem with silting was tackled by Sir Ralph Delaval in the early 1670s. He built a pier and arranged for sea water to be trapped behind a sluice at each high tide. At low tide the sluice was opened and the harbour flushed: hence the name Seaton Sluice.

In 1812 Newcastle's castle was bought by the Corporation, and it was after this date that the corner turrets and battlements were added to the keep. The Black Gate was originally constructed in 1247, when the castle's defences were upgraded, but the house on top of the gate is a much later addition.

A coal port in the 17th century, and a 'des res' for the well-heeled of Newcastle from the late 19th century onwards, Cullercoats was also a noted fishing community. From the doors of the cottages seen in photograph C283006 (below), fisherwives in their distinctive costume sold fish.

CULLERCOATS, FISHERMEN'S COTTAGES c1955 C283006

WHITLEY BAY, SPANISH CITY c1955 W246001

Spanish City at Whitley Bay, shown in photograph W246001 (above) was built in ferro-concrete between 1908 and 1910, as a theatre and amusement arcade for Whitley Pleasure Gardens Ltd. The dome is thought to be one of the earliest ferro-concrete domes in Britain.

The coming of the railway transformed Whitley Bay into a popular tripper resort for the people of Tyneside (photograph W246007, right). Special low fares after 6.00pm brought in evening visitors by the hundreds. The railway also turned Whitley Bay into commuter country for those who could afford to escape the grime of Newcastle.

The Laing Art Gallery at New Bridge Street in Newcastle holds a collection of wood engravings and other work by Thomas Bewick (1753 - 1828), who became the most famous wood-engraver in the world. Bewick was apprenticed at the age of fourteen to Ralph Beilby, an engraver in Newcastle who did all kinds of work, from printing bank notes to etching initials on silver, and was trained to be a wood-engraver, an art which at that time produced coarse and crude prints used mainly for the most basic ornaments and roughest designs. At the end of his apprenticeship, Bewick moved to London and fame, but could not settle in the capital and returned to Newcastle, where he formed a partnership with his former master, Beilby. Bewick transformed the art of wood-engraving into the most popular form of graphic art in England until the introduction of photography in the later 19th century. His technique involved engraving the end (instead of the length) of the wood, which resulted in a finer grain. His further innovation was to cut in plain parallel lines instead of cross-lines. This technique, called 'white-line engraving', means that more or less wood is cut away to show different amounts of light and shade when the wood is inked and impressed on paper, resulting in a much more sophisticated print.

WHITLEY BAY, SOUTH LOWER PROMENADE c1955 W246007

JARROW, ST PAUL'S CHURCH c1965 J5015

The Saxon St Paul's Church at Jarrow (photograph J5015, above) dates from before AD684, and its inscribed dedication still remains. The tower was built in the late 11th century.

In the centre of the new Dockwray Square in North Shields is a statue of the famous comedian Stan Laurel, one half of the comedy duo Laurel and Hardy, who spent part of his childhood here. Stan's father, A J Jefferson, became manager of the Theatre Royal in North Shields c1900, and the family lived at No 8 in the old Dockwray Square (this has now been replaced by Nos 6-7). A blue plaque marks the location of Stan Laurel's former home.

The liner 'Mauretania', which held the record for the fastest Atlantic crossing for 22 years, was launched from Wallsend in 1907.

Though originally only a couple of miles to the north of Newcastle, Gosforth had a character and identity of its own. Every year during the last week in June the town would be packed with people for Race Week and the running of the Northumberland Plate. In 1947 over 57,000 punters flocked to Newcastle Races on Plate Day to see the first running of the race since 1939 and the dark days of the Second World War.

GOSFORTH, HIGH STREET 1956 G125008

The Roman fort of Segedunum once stood at Wallsend, at the eastern end of Hadrian's Wall. Between 1870 and 1914, Wallsend's population rocketed from 10,400 to over 41,000. Land was needed for housing, and nothing was sacred. Even the ruins of Segedunum had to go, although not without a fight. William Boyd, the borough's first mayor, attempted to organise a fund to buy the field in which the remains of the Roman fort stood. The owners wanted £680, which Boyd did not have - but the builders did. The builders moved in and destroyed what was left of the old fort; the rubble was used for the roads.

In 1973 a large quantity of fragments of wooden tablets covered with writing were found at Vindolanda, one of the forts on Hadrian's Wall. The fragments were found to be an assortment of letters from home, administrative records, and other 'trivia' - even an invitation to a birthday party from the wife of one commanding officer to another. The tablets are full of the small details of everyday service on the Wall, and provide a fascinating insight to the lives of those lonely men on their windswept hills, which must have seemed like a posting to the end of the known world. One mother wrote to her soldier son: 'I have sent you ... pairs of socks, two pairs of sandals and two pairs of underpants.' The 20th-century poet W H Auden imagined what the Wall posting might have felt like in his poem 'Roman Wall Blues':

> *Over the heather the wet wind blows,*
> *I've lice in my tunic and cold in my nose.*
> *The rain comes pattering out of the sky,*
> *I'm a wall soldier, I don't know why.*

**SOUTH SHIELDS,
MARKET PLACE
1902** S162009

NEWCASTLE, THE QUAYSIDE 1896 N16320

In photograph N16320 (above), the late 19th-century skyline of
Newcastle is dominated by the 15th-century tower and spire of
St Nicholas's Cathedral and the imposing bulk of the castle keep.
Also featured are the Moot Hall, built 1810-12, and the much older
Guildhall, which was completely rebuilt by Robert Trollop in 1655-58
and extended by John Dobson.

Each section of Hadrian's Wall contains a plaque engraved with the
details of the unit and centurion in charge of construction. Along
Hadrian's Wall there are also many carvings and engravings left by
the legionaries and their followers whilst they were stationed on
the Wall. Some of the carvings are of Roman gods and symbols of
worship, while others are more phallic!

When the late 18th-century bridge over the Tyne at Newcastle was demolished in the 1870s to make way for the Swing Bridge, traces of an earlier medieval bridge (destroyed by flood in 1771) and a Roman bridge were discovered. The Swing Bridge cost £228,000 to build. It has an overall length of 560ft; the swing section is 281ft, giving two navigable channels each 104ft wide. The superstructure was designed and built by Sir W G Armstrong at Elswick and was floated into place.

Mosley Street in Newcastle was the first street in the world to be lit by electricity.

NEWCASTLE, THE SWING BRIDGE 1890 N16318

NEWCASTLE, GREY STREET 1900 N16321

The Victorian music hall song called 'The Blaydon Races' which has become the Geordieland 'national anthem' was written by a Gateshead man, George Ridley. The first public performance of the song was in 1862 at a testimonial for the Tyneside rowing hero, Harry Clasper. The song descibes a coach journey from Newcastle to the races at Blaydon. Most of the events in the song actually happened in the races of 1861, although the storm referred to in the last verse occurred in 1862, and prevented the horses reaching the racecourse on an island in the Tyne.

In St Nicholas's Cathedral in Newcastle is a magnificent memorial brass of 1441. It is one of the largest in the country, and commemorates Roger Thornton and his wife, Agnes, and their many children. Roger Thornton was a 'Dick Whittington-style' self-made man who arrived in the town with nothing, but went on to become a successful merchant; he was also Lord Mayor of Newcastle three times. A local rhyme said:

> *'In at the Westgate came Thornton in*
> *with a happen hapt in a ram's skin.'*

In the late 18th century, Wallsend's local church of Holy Cross at Willington Gut was roofless and unusable. The schoolroom was pressed into service as a replacement church, and all went well for about 10 years. Then in 1806 the Dean and Chapter caused chaos and alarm by announcing that, as the schoolroom had never been consecrated, all weddings that had taken place there were invalid. Even worse, all the couples that had 'married' there were technically living in sin, and all children born to them were illegitimate. The result was the building of St Peter's, in some haste, on the hill above the local ropeworks.

NEWCASTLE, THE EARL GREY MONUMENT c1955 N16011

GRAINGER STREET 1900 N16314

Grainger Street in Newcastle (photograph N16314, above) is named after one of the three prominent 19th-century citizens who were responsible for much of the town centre. Richard Grainger and John Dobson supplied the architectural talent, and John Clayton the money and influence. These men planned and built one of the finest town centres in England, favouring the elegant and graceful Classical style instead of the Gothic Revival that was so fashionable with other Victorian architects. Their choice has stood the test of time.

Hadrian's Wall was designated a World Heritage Site in 1987, making it one of 721 world treasures alongside the Taj Mahal, the Great Wall of China and Stonehenge.

In 1852 the Jarrow shipbuilding yard of Palmer Bros turned out the world's first sea-going screw collier for the mine owner John Bowes of Barnard Castle. Carrying 650 tonnes of coal per trip, she could do the work of eight sailing colliers.

Laygate Lane, shown in photograph S162001, below, is one of a number of sturdy Victorian terraces in South Shields; many of them were built speculatively by developers as the town expanded thanks to its coal and alkali industries.

SOUTH SHIELDS, LAYGATE LANE 1900 S162001

SOUTH SHIELDS, FREDERICK STREET c1906 S162002

During the first half of the 19th century a number of churches were built to meet the needs of the growing population of South Shields. The Presbyterian Church, Frederick Street, was built in 1847; Holy Trinity, Laygate, was earlier, having been built in 1832-34 to the designs of Anthony Salvin. Both have since been demolished.

The architect John Dobson's porticoed Central Station in Newcastle is his masterpiece, a monument to the railway age that is most appropriate to Newcastle since the railway pioneer George Stephenson was born in the village of Wylam, eight miles from the city. A statue of Stephenson stands in Westgate Road, near the station.

In 1903, the company of Swan, Hunter & Wigham Richardson was formed at Wallsend from the amalgamation of the yards of Charles Swan & Hunter and Wigham Richardson & Co. The new shipbuilding giant also purchased the intervening yard of the Tyne Ship and Pontoon Co to give a continuous frontage, and took a majority holding in the marine engineering firm Wallsend Slipway and Engineering.

Photograph N16303 (below) shows a street scene with road works 19th-century style to the left, and a water cart to the right. Water carts were used to dampen down the streets, in an effort to settle the dust and combat the daily stench created by the large amounts of horse-droppings that were deposited on the streets every day.

NEWCASTLE c1890 N16303

25

An example of the proud shipbuilding tradition of Tyneside can be seen in this photograph, showing the 'Empress of England' leaving Liverpool; this vessel was built in 1957 by Vickers-Armstrong of Newcastle. Originally intended to run the liner service from Liverpool to Quebec and Montreal in summer and Liverpool to St John's in winter, she began to spend her winters cruising in the Caribbean from New York as air travel hit the American market, a development which hit the shipbuilding industry very hard. After a refit in the early 1970s she was renamed the 'Ocean Monarch', but was scrapped in 1975.

THE 'EMPRESS OF ENGLAND' LEAVING LIVERPOOL c1958 L60034

Bede's chair in St Paul's Church, Jarrow, is traditionally thought to have belonged to the Venerable Bede (AD673-735), the chronicler monk who spent most of his life in the monastery at Jarrow. For centuries, this ancient oak chair was popularly believed to influence marriage and childbirth. Unmarried girls placed splinters from the chair beneath their pillows so that they would dream of their future husbands. Brides sat in it after the wedding ceremony to ensure fertility, while mothers-to-be soaked wood chips carved from the chair in water and then drank the liquid in the hope that it would ease the pangs of childbirth.

Although there was a glass manufacturing industry at Wallsend in the 17th century, the town owed its development to coal and shipbuilding. Wallsend Colliery was started by a Quaker family, but they ran into financial difficulties; they borrowed money from a Sunderland timber merchant by the name of William Russell, but as soon as the pit shaft was sunk, Russell foreclosed the mortgage and took over the pit. Eventually Russell owned seven pits around Wallsend, and made enough money to buy Brancepeth Castle. The last pit in the town, Rising Sun Colliery, was proclaimed by the NCB to be one of its long-life pits, yet it was closed in 1969 and demolished in 1974.

North Shields once had an important fishing industry; along with Blyth and Newbiggin, it was one of the top ports for white fish such as cod, haddock, whiting, ling, halibut, sole, catfish, dab, plaice, conger eel, coalfish and skate, as well as catches of mackerel, crabs, lobsters and periwinkles. In the early 1920s there were nearly 60 trawlers operating out of North Shields; Richard Irwin & Sons were at their peak in 1939, with a fleet of 39 vessels.

SOUTH SHIELDS, MARSDEN BAY c1955 S162303

Jarrow was the home of the famous shipbuilding yard of Palmer Bros, founded in 1851 by the brothers Charles and George Palmer to build colliers to ship coal to London. The firm expanded rapidly, acquiring fourteen of its own coalmines as well as its own ironstone company, and also interests in firms that supplied ships fittings. From 1860 until 1912 Palmers also operated a yard at Howdon, where a considerable number of ships were built. After George Palmer retired, Charles continued to develop the business, opening an engine works, blast furnaces and iron and steel works. The company, which went public in 1865, was always innovative. In 1906 electric overhead cranes were installed, and in 1911 the seven-berth Hebburn yard of Robert Stephenson & Sons was leased and eventually purchased. Other acquisitions included a small yard at Amble and the building of a dry dock at Swansea for Palmers (Swansea) Dry Dock Co.

WALLSEND, HIGH STREET c1955 W168001

In 1930 the output from British shipbuilding yards totalled 1.4 million tonnes. By 1933, as the Depression hit, it had slumped to 133,000 tonnes. Palmers of Jarrow completed their last merchant ship order in April 1931 and their last warship in 1933. With no prospect of further orders, the company went into liquidation in 1935. It was a complete closure: shipyard, blast furnaces, rolling mills and engine works. Palmers passed into the hands of the National Shipbuilders' Security, a controversial organisation set up by the industry to administer self-inflicted surgery to reduce shipbuilding capacity. Yards were bought and then demolished. The owners were compensated, but their former employees got nothing. The effect upon Jarrow was disastrous: with no help forthcoming from the Government of the day, the town was left with the highest rate of unemployment in the country.

The world's only bagpipe museum, which was formerly housed in the Black Gate at Newcastle's castle, has now been moved to new premises at Morpeth, a few miles up the A1. More than 100 different sets of bagpipes from all over the world can be seen, including the local Northumbrian pipes. These are blown by a bellows tucked under the piper's arm, unlike Scottish pipes, which are blown by mouth. The music of Northumbrian pipes has been brought to worldwide notice in recent years through the work of the renowned folk musician Kathryn Tickell.

After the collapse of the Jarrow shipbuilding industry in the 1930s the view of Walter Runciman, the President of the Board of Trade, was that 'Jarrow must work out its own salvation'. This phrase kindled a strong reaction, and 200 men set out in October 1936 to walk 300 miles to London on a hunger march that has become famous as the Jarrow Crusade. Organised by the town council and local MP Ellen Wilkinson, the Crusade was an attempt to get the Government and people in the rest of the country to take notice of the dire straits Jarrow had been left in after the closure of Palmers, and do something pro-active to attract alternative forms of industry. There was a 70% unemployment rate in Jarrow, and one of the marchers described his home town at the time as a 'filthy, dirty, falling down, consumptive area'. The men took 3 weeks and 5 days to reach London, playing mouth organs along the way to keep up their spirits. They slept in schools, drill halls and casualty wards of hospitals along the route; both Labour and Conservative organisations provided baths and hot meals, and relays of medical students cared for blistered feet and other ailments. There was widespread sympathy for the Jarrow Crusade, and the men marched into London in the pouring rain to a huge meeting in Hyde Park. A few new factories were set up in Jarrow after the march, but Jarrow's economy did not really get the boost it needed until the Second World War.

NEWCASTLE, THE SANDHILL 1894 N16319

In the centre of photograph N16319 (above), the warehouse of
J W Newton & Co can be seen. This building was formerly the house
of the banker Aubone Surtees. On the night of 18 November 1772
his daughter Bessie climbed down a ladder from one of the windows
and into the arms of her lover John Scott. The couple then fled across
the Scottish border and were married at Blackshiels, Midlothian. John
Scott later became Lord Chancellor of England.

Recorded on the grave of a Newcastle architect at Gateshead:
ROBERT TROLLOPE
Here lies Robert Trollope
Who made these stones roll up;
When death took his soul up,
His body filled this hole up.

The first Prince Bishop of Durham, William Walcher, also Earl of Northumberland, was murdered at Gateshead in 1081. One of his men murdered a popular Anglo-Saxon noble, and the bishop called a meeting at Gateshead to try and defuse high feelings. An angry mob shouted him down, and he was brutally murdered. His body was retrieved by monks from the monastery at Jarrow, and he was interred at Durham.

JARROW, GRANGE ROAD WEST c1955 J5001

Whickham was once an important economic asset to the Prince
Bishops of Durham. Coal was being extracted at a profit from the
Whickham and Gateshead area well before the end of the 13th
century, and surviving account books show that Whickham mines

WHICKHAM, THE HIGHWAY c1955 W244008

were contributing significant revenues to the bishop in the 15th and 16th centuries. At the Reformation the Church's mines were confiscated by the Crown, and were then offered on 99-year leases to Newcastle merchants.

SOUTH SHIELDS, KING STREET c1898 S162005

Love it or hate it, you can't miss the Angel of the North, the landmark sculpture commissioned by Gateshead Council to mark the entrance to Tyneside. The Angel's wide, open arms greet visitors as they reach Gateshead, whether they come by road or rail, and the huge sculpture attracts 150,000 people a year who come to view it close-up. The Angel of the North was created by the internationally renowned sculptor Antony Gormley from 200 tonnes of steel. At 20m (65ft) high, it is more than the height of four double-decker buses, and its wingspan is 54m (175) wide.

The Gateshead Millennium Bridge, a foot and cycle bridge spanning the River Tyne between Gateshead and Newcastle, was lifted into place in November 2000 by one of the world's largest floating cranes, and was opened to the public on 17 September 2001. The bridge, which cost £22 million to build, has become a tourist attraction renowned for its elegance and beauty. Huge hydraulic rams on each side of the bridge allow it to tilt back on special pivots, allowing river traffic on the Tyne to pass underneath. This manoeuvre has led to it being nicknamed the Blinking Eye Bridge.

NEWCASTLE, THE CASTLE 1901 N16322

SOUTH SHIELDS, KING STREET 1906 S162003X

From its earliest times, Gateshead has been sited on an ancient routeway, and in Roman times a road ran through the area. Part of this Roman road may have followed the course of the modern High Street of the town. The position of Gateshead at the head of an important road or 'gate' from the south has led some people to suggest this as the derivation of the town name. However, an alternative explanation for the name is that it may be a reference to wild goats which used to frequent the area; this interpretation is supported by the writings of the 7th-century monk, the Venerable Bede, who described the area in Latin as 'Ad Caprae Caput', which means 'the Goats' Head'. The Venerable Bede referred to 'Ad Caprae Caput' (Gateshead) as the site of a monastery, which was under the rule of Abbot Utta in AD653. Very little else is known about the Gateshead area in Anglo-Saxon times.

One of Newcastle's best-kept secrets is the Victoria Tunnel, which was built between 1839-42 to house a wagonway to transport coal from the Spital Tongues colliery to the ships waiting on the River Tyne. Newcastle's town council refused permission for a wagonway to be built through the town centre, so the mine owners decided to take it underground through a specially built tunnel instead. The coal was loaded into wheeled wagons which ran along rails on the floor of the tunnel. The wagonway was in operation until the closure of the pit which used it, c1860, after which the tunnel was unused for over 80 years. However, it was reopened for use as an air raid shelter during the Second World War, as it was deep enough to be bomb-proof. New entrances were made, and basic amenities were provided to make it a safe haven for 9,000 people.

NEWCASTLE, GREY STREET 1890 N16317

Recorded on a tombstone in a Newcastle cemetery:
Here lies a man, who all his mortal life,
Spent mending clocks, but could not mend his wife.
The alarm of his bell was never so shrill,
As was her tongue clacking like a mill.
But now he's gone - of whither none can tell -
I hope beyond the sound of his wife's yell.

In the early hours of 6 October 1854, a worsted factory close to the River Tyne in Hillgate, Gateshead, caught fire. The fire quickly spread to an adjacent warehouse which contained large quantities of salt, iron, lead, manganese, nitrate of soda, guano, arsenic, copperas, naptha, and 3,000 tonnes of brimstone. This mixture caused the building to explode; the sound of the explosion was heard as far away as Berwick upon Tweed. The flaming debris caused many boats on the Tyne to catch fire, and also caused a second conflagration to break out on the northern bank of the Tyne, destroying many medieval buildings on Newcastle's quayside. The event became known as the Great Fire of Newcastle and Gateshead; it made hundreds of people homeless, and destroyed nearly all the historic buildings in Gateshead.

Outside the Civic Centre in Newcastle is the striking and unusual war memorial which commemorates the response from local men to the call to arms of the First World War. The moving bronze relief shows women and children waving goodbye to their loved ones, a scene that would have been familiar to people from all walks of life throughout the city. The monument was designed by William Goscombe John RA, and was described by Alan Borg, former Director General of the Imperial War Museum, as 'one of the finest sculptural ensembles on any British monument'.

Attached to the exterior wall of Newcastle's Civic Centre is a bronze figure that represents the River God of the Tyne; his head is bowed and a stream of water flows from his raised right arm. The figure was created in 1968 by David Wynne, and is his interpretation of a stone carving of a figure of the Tyne River God dating from 1786 on the wall of Somerset House in London. The original figure, which was part of a series of eight carvings representing the most important rivers in the country, had fish tangled in his hair and held picks and baskets of coal, which represented the trade and industry of the Tyne in the late 18th century.

JARROW, GRANGE ROAD WEST c1955 J5004

SPORTING NEWCASTLE
AND TYNESIDE

Exotic foreign football stars are nothing new in Newcastle. As far back as 1951, Newcastle United had a Chilean international player gracing the team. He was George Robledo, who scored 91 goals in 166 games, including the winning goal in the 1952 FA Cup final against Arsenal.

Andrew Stoddart, born in South Shields in 1863, holds the rare distinction of captaining England at both rugby and cricket. He came late to cricket, not playing the game seriously until the age of 22. He played on four tours of Australia, in 1894-95 and 1897-98. Among his other achievements was a score of 485, playing for Hampstead, in 1886; this was the highest ever recorded score at the time. Stoddart also captained the England rugby team on the 1887-88 tour of Australia. In all, he played rugby ten times for his country.

The tragic death of Jarrow-born Jimmy Thorpe lead to major changes in the rules of football. The brilliant goalkeeper was the first-choice keeper for Sunderland in the early 1930s. During a game against Chelsea in February 1936 he was repeatedly kicked whilst holding the ball, and sadly died from his injuries. The authorities quickly changed the rules to stop outfield players raising their foot to the goalkeeper when he is holding the ball.

Boxing was big business in pre-Second World War Newcastle. At least 38 different venues staged the sport between 1886 and 1933, and in the 1930s a purpose-built stadium, the New St James Hall, was built. In its heyday, 1933-34, six professional promotions were staged each week. One of the most notable fighters from the area was Mickey Maguire from Byker. He turned professional at fifteen years of age, and once beat the World Flyweight Champion, Victor Perez of Tunisia. Sadly, the victory was in a non-title fight, and Maguire retired aged 25, never having fought for a world title.

It is not perhaps widely known that during the mid 19th century there was a flourishing professional rowing circuit in the area. The top rowers were big stars, and the Newcastle area produced three important figures in the sport, who regularly rowed in front of crowds of up to 100,000 on the Tyne. James Renforth, who grew up in Gateshead, was a highly talented rower who won considerable sums of money; for instance, in January 1871 he won £400 in a race on the Tyne (to give an idea of value, this would have been four times a teacher's annual salary in those days). Renforth died young, at the age of 29, whilst competing at an event in Canada. The town of Renforth in Canada is named in his honour. Two other prominent local rowers of the time were Henry Clasper and Robert Chambers. Clasper had a long and distinguished career; testament of this was the crowd of over 130,000 that lined his funeral route in 1870. Chambers's claims to fame include winning the first 'world professional sculling contest' in 1863, a match worth thousands of pounds.

The north-east's tradition of athletic success in road and track racing is not confined to recent times. The success of local sporting heroes such as Brendan Foster and Steve Cram along with the huge popularity of the Great North Run were preceded by the long history of the Morpeth Road Race. This race, of approximately 14 miles between Morpeth and Newcastle, was run for 100 years from 1904 to 2004, and was claimed to be the oldest road race in Britain.

QUIZ QUESTIONS

Answers on page 50.

1. What was the Roman name for Newcastle?

2. Which former resident of Jarrow was responsible for devising our dating system?

3. Who was 'Red Ellen'?

4. Who is commemorated by the monument in Newcastle's Grey Street, and why?

5. In St Nicholas's Cathedral in Newcastle is a memorial brass to Roger Thornton and his wife Agnes. How many children did Agnes bear her husband?

6. At the western end of the Newcastle quayside is a street called Sandgate. This street was the area where the keelmen lived - who were the keelmen?

7. The best-selling author Catherine Cookson was born in Tyne Dock, South Shields in 1906. Her books are loved by millions, but she also wrote novels under another name - what was it?

8. Which extremely useful device was invented by Gladstone Adams, who was born at 4 St Anne's Row in Newcastle on 16 May 1880?

9. In the vicinity of City Road you can see the remains of one of the seventeen towers that guarded the town wall around medieval Newcastle. This tower has a small gateway called the Sally Port - why was it called this?

10. What was the name of the popular children's television series set in a Newcastle youth club?

NEWCASTLE, HEATON PARK c1884 17000

RECIPE

Bacon Floddies are a traditional dish from Gateshead. They can be served on their own, but are usually served with sausages or bacon and eggs for breakfast or supper.

BACON FLODDIES

Ingredients

225g/8oz peeled potatoes
2 medium onions, peeled
175g/6oz bacon rashers, finely chopped
50g/2oz self-raising flour

Salt and freshly ground black pepper
2 eggs, beaten
4 tablespoons bacon dripping or oil

Grate the potatoes and onion into a mixing bowl. Add the finely chopped bacon, the flour and the seasoning and mix well. Add the beaten eggs, mixing them well through all the ingredients. Heat the dripping or oil in a heavy pan until hot but not smoking. Add tablespoons of the floddies to the pan, not overcrowding them, and fry carefully on both sides until they are golden and cooked through. Drain on paper towels and keep hot in a dish until ready to serve.

GATESHEAD, SALTWELL PARK LAKE c1955 G124001

RECIPE

PAN HAGGERTY

This is a traditional dish from Northumberland.

Ingredients

60ml/4 tablespoons oil
450g/1lb firm potatoes, thinly sliced

1 large onion, thinly sliced
115g/4oz grated mature Cheddar cheese
Salt and pepper

Heat the oil in a large, heavy frying pan. Remove the pan from the heat and arrange alternate layers of potato, onion and cheese, starting with a layer of potatoes and seasoning each layer. Return the pan to the heat, and cook for 30 minutes, starting over a low heat and gradually increasing it so that the underside of the mixture browns. Switch on the grill, and when good and hot place the pan under the grill for 5-10 minutes to brown the top of the mixture. Slide the Pan Haggerty on to a warm plate and serve cut into wedges.

QUIZ ANSWERS

1. Pons Aelius. There was a Roman bridge here; 'Pons' means bridge, and 'Aelius' was the family name of the emperor who gave his name to Hadrian's Wall, so the name can be translated as 'The Bridge of Hadrian'.

2. The Venerable Bede (AD673-735), a monk who lived and worked at the Anglo-Saxon monastery which was near St Paul's Church in Jarrow. Bede was responsible for devising the AD and BC dating system, for dates before and after the birth of Christ.

3. 'Red Ellen' was Ellen Wilkinson, the local MP who helped organise the Jarrow Crusade in 1936, when 200 men from Jarrow marched 300 miles to London in an attempt to raise awareness about unemployment in the town.

4. The monument in Grey Street (photograph N16011, page 21) commemorates Earl Grey (1764-1845), who was the MP for Northumberland for more than 20 years and also the Prime Minister who masterminded the Reform Bill of 1832. This important piece of legislation gave seats in Parliament to the new towns created by the Industrial Revolution. It was a reform that had been strongly resisted by the more reactionary element of British society, and was achieved after over 50 years of agitation from people who felt that those who were creating the wealth of the country should be represented in its Parliament.

5. Seven sons and seven daughters.

6. The keelmen were unique to the Tyneside region. They were highly skilled boatmen, who handled the movement of coal from the riverside to the ships waiting on the Tyne. The keelmen took their name from their small vessels, called keels, which could carry around 20 tonnes of coal. The first recorded use of keels for transporting coal on the Tyne comes from the early 1300s. The keelmen thought of themselves as a separate community, and wore a distinctive blue jacket, along with a yellow waistcoat, flared trousers and a black silk hat tied with a ribbon.

7.   Catherine Cookson, who died in 1998, also wrote popular novels under the name of Catherine Marchant.

8.   In April 1911 Gladstone Adams patented a device with the Liverpool Patent Office for cleaning the windscreens of motorcars, which could be operated by either hand or foot and had a vertical movement. Adams was the first person to register this invention - although Prince Henry of Russia claimed that he had invented a similar device, he did not register it until later in the same year. The world's first windscreen wiper is now in the collection of the Discovery Museum in Newcastle, and was featured in the BBC TV programme 'Local Heroes', presented by Adam Hart-Davis.

9.   The Sally Port was the gateway from which the defenders of Newcastle would 'sally forth' out of the town against the enemy.

10. 'Byker Grove'.

SOUTH SHIELDS, FOWLER STREET c1900 S162006

NEWCASTLE, THE QUAYSIDE 1928 N16316

E.W. YOUNGE
TRANSPORT SPE

XN-5

FRANCIS FRITH

PIONEER VICTORIAN PHOTOGRAPHER

Francis Frith, founder of the world-famous photographic archive, was a complex and multi-talented man. A devout Quaker and a highly successful Victorian businessman, he was philosophical by nature and pioneering in outlook. By 1855 he had already established a wholesale grocery business in Liverpool, and sold it for the astonishing sum of £200,000, which is the equivalent today of over £15,000,000. Now in his thirties, and captivated by the new science of photography, Frith set out on a series of pioneering journeys up the Nile and to the Near East.

INTRIGUE AND EXPLORATION

He was the first photographer to venture beyond the sixth cataract of the Nile. Africa was still the mysterious 'Dark Continent', and Stanley and Livingstone's historic meeting was a decade into the future. The conditions for picture taking confound belief. He laboured for hours in his wicker dark-room in the sweltering heat of the desert, while the volatile chemicals fizzed dangerously in their trays. Back in London he exhibited his photographs and was 'rapturously cheered' by members of the Royal Society. His reputation as a photographer was made overnight.

VENTURE OF A LIFE-TIME

By the 1870s the railways had threaded their way across the country, and Bank Holidays and half-day Saturdays had been made obligatory by Act of Parliament. All of a sudden the working man and his family were able to enjoy days out, take holidays, and see a little more of the world.

With typical business acumen, Francis Frith foresaw that these new tourists would enjoy having souvenirs to commemorate their days out. For the next thirty years he travelled the country by train and by pony and trap, producing fine photographs of seaside resorts and beauty spots that were keenly bought by millions of Victorians. These prints were painstakingly pasted into family albums and pored over during the dark nights of winter, rekindling precious memories of summer excursions. Frith's studio was soon supplying retail shops all over the country, and by 1890 F Frith & Co had become the greatest specialist photographic publishing company in the world, with over 2,000 sales outlets, and pioneered the picture postcard.

FRANCIS FRITH'S LEGACY

Francis Frith had died in 1898 at his villa in Cannes, his great project still growing. By 1970 the archive he created contained over a third of a million pictures showing 7,000 British towns and villages.

Frith's legacy to us today is of immense significance and value, for the magnificent archive of evocative photographs he created provides a unique record of change in the cities, towns and villages throughout Britain over a century and more. Frith and his fellow studio photographers revisited locations many times down the years to update their views, compiling for us an enthralling and colourful pageant of British life and character.

We are fortunate that Frith was dedicated to recording the minutiae of everyday life. For it is this sheer wealth of visual data, the painstaking chronicle of changes in dress, transport, street layouts, buildings, housing and landscape that captivates us so much today, offering us a powerful link with the past and with the lives of our ancestors.

Computers have now made it possible for Frith's many thousands of images to be accessed almost instantly. The archive offers every one of us an opportunity to examine the places where we and our families have lived and worked down the years. Its images, depicting our shared past, are now bringing pleasure and enlightenment to millions around the world a century and more after his death.

For further information visit: www.francisfrith.com

INTERIOR DECORATION

Frith's photographs can be seen framed and as giant wall murals in thousands of pubs, restaurants, hotels, banks, retail stores and other public buildings throughout Britain. These provide interesting and attractive décor, generating strong local interest and acting as a powerful reminder of gentler days in our increasingly busy and frenetic world.

FRITH PRODUCTS

All Frith photographs are available as prints and posters in a variety of different sizes and styles. In the UK we also offer a range of other gift and stationery products illustrated with Frith photographs, although many of these are not available for delivery outside the UK – see our web site for more information on the products available for delivery in your country.

THE INTERNET

Over 100,000 photographs of Britain can be viewed and purchased on the Frith web site. The web site also includes memories and reminiscences contributed by our customers, who have personal knowledge of localities and of the people and properties depicted in Frith photographs. If you wish to learn more about a specific town or village you may find these reminiscences fascinating to browse. Why not add your own comments if you think they would be of interest to others? See **www.francisfrith.com**

PLEASE HELP US BRING FRITH'S PHOTOGRAPHS TO LIFE

Our authors do their best to recount the history of the places they write about. They give insights into how particular towns and villages developed, they describe the architecture of streets and buildings, and they discuss the lives of famous people who lived there. But however knowledgeable our authors are, the story they tell is necessarily incomplete.

Frith's photographs are so much more than plain historical documents. They are living proofs of the flow of human life down the generations. They show real people at real moments in history; and each of those people is the son or daughter of someone, the brother or sister, aunt or uncle, grandfather or grandmother of someone else. All of them lived, worked and played in the streets depicted in Frith's photographs.

We would be grateful if you would give us your insights into the places shown in our photographs: the streets and buildings, the shops, businesses and industries. Post your memories of life in those streets on the Frith website: what it was like growing up there, who ran the local shop and what shopping was like years ago; if your workplace is shown tell us about your working day and what the building is used for now. Read other visitors' memories and reconnect with your shared local history and heritage. With your help more and more Frith photographs can be brought to life, and vital memories preserved for posterity, and for the benefit of historians in the future.

Wherever possible, we will try to include some of your comments in future editions of our books. Moreover, if you spot errors in dates, titles or other facts, please let us know, because our archive records are not always completely accurate—they rely on 140 years of human endeavour and hand-compiled records. You can email us using the contact form on the website.

Thank you!

For further information, trade, or author enquiries
please contact us at the address below:

The Francis Frith Collection, Oakley Business Park, Wylye Road, Dinton, Wiltshire SP3 5EU.
Tel: +44 (0)1722 716 376 Fax: +44 (0)1722 716 881
e-mail: sales@francisfrith.co.uk **www.francisfrith.com**